UNIVERSITY OF UTAH®
UTES™
COOKBOOK

JENNY AHLSTROM STANGER

PHOTOGRAPHS BY ZAC WILLIAMS

GIBBS SMITH
TO ENRICH AND INSPIRE HUMANKIND

First Edition
14 13 12 11 10   5 4 3 2 1

Text © 2010 Jenny Ahlstrom Stanger
Photographs © 2010 Zac Williams

Published by
Gibbs Smith
P.O. Box 667
Layton, Utah 84041

1.800.835.4993 orders
www.gibbs-smith.com

Designed by Dawn DeVries Sokol
Printed and bound in China
Gibbs Smith books are printed on either recycled, 100% post-consumer waste,
FSC-certified papers or on paper produced from a 100% certified sustainable
forest/controlled wood source.

Library of Congress Cataloging-in-Publication Data

Stanger, Jenny Ahlstrom.
  University of Utah Utes cookbook / Jenny Ahlstrom Stanger ; photographs by
Zac Williams. — 1st ed.
    p. cm.
  ISBN-13: 978-1-4236-1646-7
  ISBN-10: 1-4236-1646-4
  1. Cookery. 2. Cookery—Utah. I. Utah Utes (Football team) II. Title.
TX714.S73846 2010
  641.59792—dc22
                        2010005869

CONTENTS

Shining Star
SALSA

4 cups diced fresh
   pineapple

4 medium tomatoes,
   seeded and diced

1½ cups diced red onion

1½ cups minced
   fresh cilantro, plus
   more for garnish

2 jalapeños, seeded
   and diced (or 3
   teaspoons crushed
   red pepper flakes)

2 tablespoons olive oil

2 teaspoons ground
   coriander

1½ teaspoons
   ground cumin

1 teaspoon salt

1 teaspoon minced garlic

1 tablespoon lime zest

Serves 10

Mix together all of the ingredients in a bowl and stir. Chill until serving time. Serve with red and white tortilla chips in an upside down football helmet and garnish with cilantro.

Mighty Ute™
MEATBALLS

1½ pounds ground beef

2 large eggs

1 cup grated Parmigiano-
Reggiano cheese

2 tablespoons parsley flakes

1 cup seasoned
breadcrumbs

1 large onion, finely diced

2 cloves garlic, minced

2 teaspoons salt

1½ cups water, divided

1 cup soy sauce

1 cup brown sugar

1 cup white sugar

½ tablespoon
minced ginger

1 green onion, chopped

1½ cloves garlic, minced

¾ cup cornstarch mixed
with 1 cup cold water

Makes 20 meatballs

Preheat oven to 350 degrees F.

In a large bowl, mix together the ground beef, eggs, cheese, parsley, and breadcrumbs. Add the onion, garlic, and salt. Use your hands to knead the mixture together. Add ½ cup water; mixture will be quite wet. Add another pinch of salt, then shape into golf ball–sized balls.

Place meatballs in a hot skillet to brown the sides. Then place them on a foil-covered baking sheet with sides and bake for about 15 minutes, or until done.

In a saucepan, mix together all of the remaining ingredients except the cornstarch mixture and stir over medium-high heat. Add the cornstarch mixture when the sauce comes to a boil; stir until sauce thickens and then remove from heat.

When the meatballs are completely cooked, pour into pan with the teriyaki sauce and stir to coat. Serve warm. Place meatballs alternately on a skewer with pieces of pineapple, if desired.

Ki-Yi
FRIES

5 cups vegetable oil

2 pounds russet
   baking potatoes

Seasoning salt

2 tablespoons BBQ sauce

2 tablespoons Miracle
   Whip or mayonnaise

Serves 8

Pour oil in a deep fryer or heavy saucepan to reach halfway up the sides of the pan and heat to 375 degrees F. While oil is heating, wash and cut the potatoes into uniform sticks, about ½ inch thick. As you go, put the cut potatoes in a bowl of cold water to keep them from turning brown.

Drain and thoroughly dry the potato sticks. This keeps the oil from splattering. Fry the potatoes in small batches for about 5 to 6 minutes, or until they are a light golden color and stiff. Remove potatoes from hot oil with a long-handled strainer and drain on brown paper bags or paper towels.

Bring oil back up to 375 degrees F. Return the potatoes to the oil in small batches and cook a second time for about 4 to 5 minutes, or until golden and crispy. Drain again on fresh paper bags or towels and then sprinkle with the seasoning salt. Serve immediately with the BBQ sauce and Miracle Whip or mayonnaise mixed together on the side.

Crunch 'Em
GREEN BEAN BITES

WASABI CUCUMBER RANCH DIP

½ cup ranch dressing

1 cucumber, peeled and seeded

2 tablespoons Miracle Whip or mayonnaise

2 teaspoons prepared horseradish

1 teaspoon cider vinegar

2 teaspoons wasabi paste

¼ cup chopped cilantro

Salt and pepper, to taste

11 ounces fresh green beans

2 eggs, beaten

1 cup milk

2 cups flour

1 tablespoon garlic salt

2 cups panko breadcrumbs

4 cups vegetable

Make the dip by combining all of the ingredients in a blender on high speed until smooth. Cover and chill; dip will thicken as it chills.

Wash and trim the green beans; set aside.

In a medium bowl, mix the eggs and milk together and then pour half into another bowl. In a third bowl, combine the flour and garlic salt. Pour the breadcrumbs into a fourth bowl.

Heat oil in a medium skillet to high heat (about 325 degrees F). Do not use olive oil.

First coat the beans in the egg mixture and then dip in the flour mixture. Dip in the egg mixture again. Then roll in the breadcrumbs until completely coated. Set the finished beans on a paper towel.

When the oil is hot, fry the coated beans in small batches for 2 minutes, or until golden brown. Drain on paper towels, and sprinkle with salt. Serve warm with the chilled dip.

Serves 8

Chopped Spinach
ARTICHOKE DIP

3 cloves garlic, minced

1 small onion, minced

1 (10-ounce) bag frozen spinach, thawed and drained

1 (14.75-ounce) jar marinated artichoke hearts, drained

2 (8-ounce) packages regular or light cream cheese

½ teaspoon oregano

½ teaspoon red pepper flakes

1 tablespoon lemon juice

½ cup grated Parmigiano-Reggiano cheese

Salt and pepper, to taste

Serves about 20

Spray a medium pot with nonstick cooking spray. Add garlic and onion and cook over medium heat until translucent.

Put spinach in a food processor and pulse a few times to chop. Add the artichokes and pulse a few more times. The mixture should be chunky. Add the spinach and artichokes to the pot, along with the cream cheese, oregano, red pepper flakes, and lemon juice. Heat until bubbly, then add cheese and salt and pepper.

Serve immediately with crusty bread or celery sticks.

Yummy Utah
SKILLET NACHOS

1 tablespoon olive oil

1 medium green bell pepper, chopped

1 small zucchini, chopped

½ cup salsa, plus more

1 (15-ounce) can chili with beans

1 bag tortilla chips

1½ cups grated Monterey Jack cheese

Sour cream

1 (2.25-ounce) can sliced black olives

Serves 4 to 5

In a 12-inch skillet, heat oil over high heat. Sauté the bell pepper and zucchini for 2 minutes. Stir in the salsa and chili and cook until hot. Remove mixture from skillet and then wipe skillet clean.

Arrange some of the tortilla chips in a single layer in the bottom of the skillet. Spoon the chili mixture over the chips. Sprinkle with cheese. Cover with a lid and cook over medium-high heat about 5 minutes, or until cheese is melted. Top with sour cream and olive slices. Serve with salsa on the side for dipping, if desired.

Champion Cheese
PULL-A-PARTS

4 (11-ounce) tubes
   refrigerated breadsticks

3 to 4 cups grated
   mozzarella cheese

½ cup garlic salt

½ cup olive oil

1 teaspoon salt

1 tablespoon dried dill

Pizza sauce or ranch
   dressing (or both)

Makes 24 breadsticks

Preheat oven to 375 degrees F.

Unroll the dough and separate breadsticks, leaving pairs of breadsticks together. Sprinkle 2 tablespoons cheese in the center of each pair of breadsticks and sprinkle with a dash of garlic salt. Fold together each pair of breadsticks lengthwise and pinch the edges to seal. Twist the stuffed breadsticks three times and place 1 inch apart on an ungreased nonstick baking sheet.

Bake for 15 to 20 minutes or until golden brown. Cool for 5 minutes before serving. Brush the tops with olive oil and sprinkle on salt, dill, and more garlic salt. Serve with warm pizza sauce or ranch dressing.

Fired-Up
CORN-ON-THE-COB

GARLIC HERB BUTTER

1 cup butter, room temperature

¼ cup each chopped fresh basil, rosemary, and sage

1 clove garlic, minced

10 ears corn

½ cup olive oil

Salt, pepper, and garlic powder, to taste

Serves 10

In a bowl, mix together the butter, basil, rosemary, and sage with an electric mixer, beating at medium speed until completely blended, about 1 to 2 minutes. Using wax paper, roll the butter into a log and then let stand for an hour in a cool place, covered, so the flavors develop; refrigerate until firm.

Preheat the grill to medium (about 350 degrees F).

Husk and wash the corn. Brush the corn with olive oil and then sprinkle with salt, pepper, and garlic powder. Place the corn on the grill and rotate every few minutes to keep it from burning. After a couple of turns, place the corn on the side of the grill so it isn't over direct heat; close the grill for 5 to 8 minutes. Corn is done when you can press a kernel and liquid shoots out.

Serve with the garlic herb butter and salt, pepper, and garlic powder on the side.

Utah Man
SLIDERS

2 pounds lean ground beef

½ cup chopped onion

½ cup chopped red or
green bell pepper

1 teaspoon garlic powder

1 tablespoon mustard

1½ cups ketchup

1 tablespoon brown sugar

Salt and pepper, to taste

20 mini hamburger
buns or dinner rolls

Makes 20 sandwiches

In a skillet over medium heat, brown the ground beef with the onion and bell pepper; drain. Stir in the garlic powder, mustard, ketchup, and brown sugar; mix thoroughly. Reduce heat, and simmer for 30 minutes. Season with salt and pepper.

Scoop 2 tablespoons of the meat mixture on each mini bun and serve.

Crimson Night
CHICKEN PUFFS

2 (11-ounce) tubes
  refrigerator
  crescent rolls

1 (10-ounce) box
  stuffing mix

2½ cups cooked and
  cubed chicken

¼ cup diced onion

½ cup diced celery

½ cup chopped dried
  cranberries

4 ounces cream cheese

½ cup sour cream

Dash of garlic powder

Salt and pepper, to taste

Serves 10

Preheat oven to 350 degrees F.

Open crescent roll tubes and unroll the dough. Press 2 dough triangles together to make a square; repeat with remaining crescents. Place the dry stuffing mix in a shallow dish.

In a bowl, stir together the remaining ingredients. Scoop a heaping teaspoonful of the mixture onto the dough squares. Fold the dough over the filling and pinch together the edges to form a pouch. Roll each "puff" in the stuffing mix and then place on a greased baking sheet.

Bake for 30 minutes or until golden brown. Serve warm.

BLT
RED POTATO SALAD

5 red potatoes

2 tablespoons olive
oil, divided

2 teaspoons dried rosemary

1 tablespoon red
wine vinegar

1 teaspoon Dijon mustard

1 clove garlic, minced

2 small cucumbers, cut
into ½-inch cubes

4 cups whole cherry
tomatoes, halved

1 cup cooked and
crumbled bacon

½ small red onion,
thinly sliced

Salt and pepper, to taste

2 heads Bibb lettuce,
leaves separated

Fresh parsley or basil,
chopped (optional)

Serves 10

Preheat oven to 425 degrees F.

Cut the potatoes into 1-inch cubes; set aside.

In a bowl, whisk together 1 tablespoon olive oil and rosemary; stir in the potato cubes until coated. Place potato cubes on a foil-covered baking sheet. Bake for 20 minutes or until tender, turning once.

In a bowl, whisk together the remaining olive oil, vinegar, mustard, and garlic. Add the cucumbers, tomatoes, bacon, onion, and cooked potatoes; toss to coat. Let stand for about 10 minutes. Separate the lettuce leaves to form a bed for the potato salad. Spoon the salad on top and garnish with the parsley or basil.

Red Rock
CHILI CHEESE DOGS

2 (16-ounce) cans
   chili with beans

1 (15-ounce) can cheddar
   cheese soup, condensed

¼ cup diced onion

10 hot dogs

10 hot dog buns,
   split and toasted

2 cups coarsely crushed
   tortilla chips

Grated cheese

Serves 10

In a large saucepan, combine the chili, cheese soup, and onion. Add the hot dogs; heat to boiling and then simmer for 5 minutes. Place a hot dog on each toasted bun and then top with extra chili cheese sauce. Sprinkle with chips and cheese.

Mountain West™
MAC & CHEESE

16 ounces elbow macaroni

4 tablespoons butter

½ cup diced onions

4 tablespoons flour

2 teaspoons salt

1 tablespoon
 Worcestershire sauce

4¼ cups whole milk

3 cups grated
 cheddar cheese

3 Roma tomatoes, diced

2 tablespoons
 butter, melted

¾ cup panko breadcrumbs

1 cup cooked and
 crumbled bacon

Serves 8

Cook macaroni according to package directions until noodles are al dente, usually 6 to 7 minutes; drain and then rinse with cold water to stop the cooking process.

Heat the butter in a medium saucepan over medium-low heat and sauté the onions until translucent. Add the flour and whisk until smooth. Add the salt and Worcestershire sauce.

Pour milk into a microwave-safe container and warm in the microwave for 1 minute. Whisk into the butter-flour mixture, stirring constantly, until thickened; turn off heat. Stir in the cheese until melted. Pour the macaroni noodles into the cheese sauce and then pour into lightly greased 9 x 13-inch pan or 8 individual ramekins.

Preheat the oven to 350 degrees F.

Place the tomatoes over the macaroni. Mix the melted butter and breadcrumbs together and sprinkle over the tomatoes. Sprinkle bacon over top. Cover and then bake for 20 minutes. Remove cover and bake 10 to 15 minutes more, or until golden brown and bubbly.

Whack-a-Coug™
WRAPS

1 (8-ounce) package
  cream cheese

6 (10-inch) whole
  wheat flour tortillas

1 pound sliced
  smoked turkey

1 (11-ounce) can
  mandarin oranges,
  drained

½ cup shredded carrots

1 red bell pepper,
  thinly sliced

2 cups fresh baby spinach

1 cup cashew pieces

Serves 6

Spread equal amounts of cream cheese over each tortilla. Top with turkey slices, mandarin oranges, carrots, bell pepper, spinach, and cashews. Tightly roll up each tortilla, wrap securely in plastic wrap, and refrigerate for 30 minutes or more.

About 10 minutes before serving, slice each wrap into 6 pieces. Secure each piece with a toothpick if desired. Lay cut side down on a large platter and serve.

BCS™ Busting
BAKED BEANS

4 slices bacon, chopped

½ medium onion, diced

1 tablespoon chopped
fresh rosemary, plus
more for garnish

1 (28-ounce) can
baked beans

¼ cup packed brown sugar

½ cup BBQ sauce

Salt and pepper, to taste

Serves 6 to 8

In a large saucepan, brown the bacon until crisp.
Add the onion and rosemary and sauté for 2
minutes. Add the beans, brown sugar, BBQ sauce,
salt, and pepper. Top with fresh rosemary and
serve warm.

Touchdown
PIZZAS

1 (8-ounce) can
   tomato sauce

1 teaspoon minced garlic

1 tablespoon Italian
   seasoning or oregano

2 (16-ounce) tubes
   refrigerator biscuits

3 cups grated
   mozzarella cheese

2 ounces pepperoni
   slices, diced

Red bell pepper
   strips (optional)

Makes 16 mini pizzas

Preheat oven to 350 degrees F.

In a saucepan, heat together the tomato sauce, garlic, and Italian seasoning until warm.

Open refrigerator biscuits and then flatten each biscuit with a rolling pin. Pinch two opposite sides to create a football shape. Top each biscuit with the sauce, cheese, pepperoni, and bell pepper strips, if desired. Bake for 15 minutes, or until cheese is golden brown. Cool for 5 minutes before serving.

Red Cream
SODA FLOAT

12 (12-ounce) cans
red cream soda

2 (½-gallon) cartons
vanilla ice cream

1 can spray whipped
cream

Red candy sprinkles

Serves 12

Drop 2 to 3 large scoops of vanilla ice cream into 12 tall glasses. Pour cans of soda over ice cream. Top with the whipped cream and sprinkles.

True Red Velvet
CUPCAKES

1½ cups sugar

1½ cups flour

1 cup cocoa powder

2 teaspoons baking powder

1 teaspoon baking soda

½ teaspoon salt

1 cup canola oil

½ cup milk

2 teaspoons plain yogurt

1½ cups beet puree

1 teaspoon balsamic vinegar

4 eggs

Cream cheese frosting

Makes 24 cupcakes

Preheat oven to 350 degrees F. Line cupcake pans with paper liners; set aside.

Whisk together the dry ingredients. In a separate bowl, mix together all of the wet ingredients except the frosting. Slowly add the dry ingredients and mix thoroughly. Pour batter into cupcake liners until ⅔ full. Bake for 15 minutes, or until a toothpick inserted in the center comes out clean. Cool on a wire rack. Top with cream cheese frosting.

"U"
SUGAR COOKIES

1 cup sugar

3 cups flour

½ teaspoon salt

1 teaspoon baking powder

1 cup shortening

½ cup sour cream

½ teaspoon baking soda

1 egg

1 teaspoon vanilla

Red royal frosting

White frosting

Makes about 1½ dozen

Preheat oven to 350 degrees F.

In a large bowl, mix together the sugar and flour. Add the salt and baking powder.

In another bowl, beat the shortening with a hand mixer. When well blended, add the sour cream and baking soda, followed by the egg and vanilla. Stir in the sugar and flour mixture. Chill dough for 15 minutes or more and then roll out and cut using a U-shaped cookie cutter, or create a U-template and cut the cookies out by hand.

Bake on a greased cookie sheet for 11 to 12 minutes and then cool on a wire rack. Frost with the red frosting and then pipe a line of white frosting around the edges.

Rice Eccles
CRISPY TREATS

Butter

2 (11-ounce) bags Kraft Caramel Bits (unwrapped caramels) or 1 (20-ounce) bag caramel squares, unwrapped

½ cup milk

8 cups crispy rice cereal

1 cup semisweet chocolate chips

½ cup red M&Ms

½ cup white M&Ms

Serves about 20

Heavily grease a 9 x 13-inch pan with the butter. Combine the caramels and milk in a large saucepan and cook over medium-low heat until the caramels are melted and the mixture is smooth. Remove from the heat and add the cereal; stir to coat. Stir in the chocolate chips. Press the mixture into the prepared pan. Sprinkle the red and white M&Ms over top and press down lightly so they stick. Refrigerate for at least an hour or until firm enough to cut.

Red Zone
ICE CREAM CAKE

25 unwrapped snack-sized Mounds candy bars

1 (6-pack) box cookie and cream ice cream sandwiches

4 cups strawberry cheesecake or strawberry ripple ice cream, softened

2 cups whipped cream

1 (10-ounce) jar strawberry preserves (optional)

Serves 10 to 12

Place 5 ice cream sandwiches into the bottom of a 10-inch springform pan. Slice the last ice cream sandwich into triangles to fill in the rounded corners in the pan. Place the Mounds candy bars around the sides of the pan and spread 4 cups of the softened ice cream over the ice cream sandwiches until evenly spread. Freeze until hard.

Remove from the freezer 10 minutes before serving. Slice into pieces and spoon a dollop of whipped cream on each piece. Top with strawberry preserves if desired, or another piece of candy. May be frozen for up to two months.

Crimson Line
COBBLER

3 (21-ounce) cans
cherry pie filling

2 cups flour

2 cups oats

2 cups brown sugar

½ teaspoon soda

½ teaspoon baking powder

½ teaspoon salt

1 cup butter or
margarine, softened

Vanilla ice cream or
whipped cream
(optional)

Serves 8 to 10

Preheat oven to 350 degrees F.

Pour the pie filling in a buttered 9 x 13-inch pan or in eight (4- to 6-ounce) individual ramekins. Mix together all of the remaining ingredients except the ice cream or whipped cream with a pastry blender or two forks. Sprinkle over pie filling.

Bake the 9 x 13-inch pan for 45 minutes, or the individual ramekins for 25 minutes. Serve hot with vanilla ice cream or whipped cream, if desired.

#1 Peanut Butter
BROWNIE SUNDAES

½ cup peanut butter

⅓ cup butter or
   margarine, softened

⅔ cup white sugar

½ cup packed brown sugar

2 eggs

½ teaspoon vanilla extract

1 cup flour

1 teaspoon baking powder

¼ teaspoon salt

Vanilla ice cream

Hot fudge

Whipped cream

Red and white sprinkles

Maraschino cherries

Serves 16

Preheat oven to 350 degrees F.

In a medium bowl, cream together the peanut butter and margarine. Blend in the sugars, eggs, and vanilla. Add the flour, baking powder, and salt. Pour into a greased 9 x 13-inch baking pan and bake for 30 to 35 minutes, or until the top springs back when touched. Cool, and cut into 16 squares.

Serve topped with vanilla ice cream, hot fudge, whipped cream, sprinkles, and a maraschino cherry.

Crunch the
COUGARS™ NUT MIX

2 pounds roasted salted peanuts

2 cups sugar

1 cup water

1 cup red M&Ms

1 cup white M&Ms

Serves 10

Preheat oven to 325 degrees F.

In a large saucepan, combine the nuts, sugar, and water and bring to a boil over medium-high heat. Stir frequently using a long-handled spoon once the mixture starts boiling. Once the mixture starts to boil, reduce heat to low. Cook on low heat for 30 to 35 minutes, or until the mixture is dry (no longer wet and sticky) and the peanuts resemble sugar-coated nuts.

Pour nuts on two foil-lined baking sheets and bake for 15 minutes. Toss cooled nuts with the M&Ms and store in a dry place for up to two weeks.

Ute™ POPS

3 cups red juice
  (raspberry, cherry,
  cranberry, etc.)

12 (3-ounce) paper cups
  and Popsicle sticks

3 cups white juice
  (lemonade, coconut
  juice drink, white
  grape juice, etc.)

Makes 12 popsicles

Pour 2 tablespoons red juice into each paper cup. Freeze 2 to 3 hours until firm or slushy. Remove from freezer and poke a Popsicle stick into the center of each. Add 2 tablespoons white juice and freeze 2 to 3 hours. Remove from freezer. Top off with red juice and freeze 1 to 2 hours more, or until hard. Peel off paper cups to serve.

NOTE: Try using other fun Popsicle molds!

Red-and-White
YOGURT PARFAITS

4 cups vanilla yogurt

4 cups granola

4 cups sliced fresh
strawberries

Serves 8

Set out 8 parfait glasses or tall dessert glasses. Spoon 4 tablespoons yogurt into each glass and smooth the surface. Sprinkle 4 tablespoons granola over top. Spoon 4 tablespoons strawberries over granola. Repeat layers to fill each glass.

Forever Red
APPLE CIDER

1 gallon apple cider

3 cinnamon sticks

2 envelopes cherry-
flavored Kool-
Aid drink mix

Place the cider and cinnamon sticks in a large saucepan. Bring to a boil, then reduce the heat to medium-low and simmer for 20 minutes. Add the beverage mix and stir to dissolve. Serve hot.

Makes 1 gallon

U of U®
FORTUNE COOKIES

2 (9-inch) refrigerated pie crusts

2 tablespoons cornstarch

32 small slips of paper

¼ cup red-colored sugar

Makes about 32 cookies

Preheat oven to 325 degrees F.

Lay a chilled 9-inch pie crust on a cornstarch-dusted surface. Cut out 3-inch circles with a round cookie cutter or drinking glass. To use all the dough, roll out the scraps with a rolling pin and cut out more circles.

Use a nontoxic marker to write "Go Utes™" or "Utes™ are #1" on the small slips of paper; fold and place one in the center of each dough circle. Fold the circle in half, then pinch, and fold the ends together to make the fortune cookie.

Brush the top of each cookie with water and then sprinkle on the red sugar sprinkles. Place the cookies on an ungreased cookie sheet sugar side up. Bake about 10 to 15 minutes, or until lightly browned; let them cool before removing from the pan.

Red-and-White
CINNAMON BEARS

1 (12-ounce) bag white
   chocolate chips

1 (18-ounce) bag
   cinnamon bears

Red sprinkles

Serves about 20

Place the chocolate chips in a microwave-safe bowl and heat in the microwave on high for 30 seconds; stir. Heat for another 30 seconds, stirring every 10 to 15 seconds until chocolate has melted.

Hold cinnamon bears by the head and dip them only half way into the chocolate. Gently lay the chocolate-dipped bears on wax paper and shake sprinkles over top; let set. Store in an airtight container.

Ute™ "Chop"
FRUIT SALAD

1 pound fresh
  strawberries, sliced
  or chopped

1 small cantaloupe, cubed

2 cups cubed fresh
  pineapple

2 bananas, sliced

1 (8-ounce) container
  frozen whipped
  topping, thawed

½ (3-ounce) box
  cherry gelatin mix

Serves 8 to 10

Mix together all of the fruit in a large bowl.
Refrigerate until ready to serve.

Whisk together the dry gelatin mix and whipped
topping until well combined; serve over the
chopped fruit.

ABOUT THE AUTHOR

A native of Orem, Utah, **Jenny Ahlstrom Stanger** has a bachelor's degree in family life education and has a passion for both family and food. For several years, she has taught culinary classes at Thanksgiving Point and other locations across Utah. Jenny also makes frequent guest chef appearances on local television shows. She is also the author of *Fabulous Freezer Meals*. Jenny enjoys teaching Zumba, traveling, reading, and spending time outdoors. She and her husband, Mark, reside in Elwood, Utah, with their four daughters.